Sports Cards

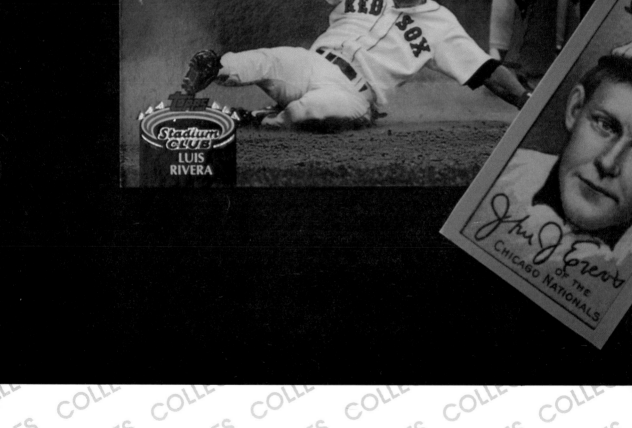

Sports Cards

By Robert Young, 1951

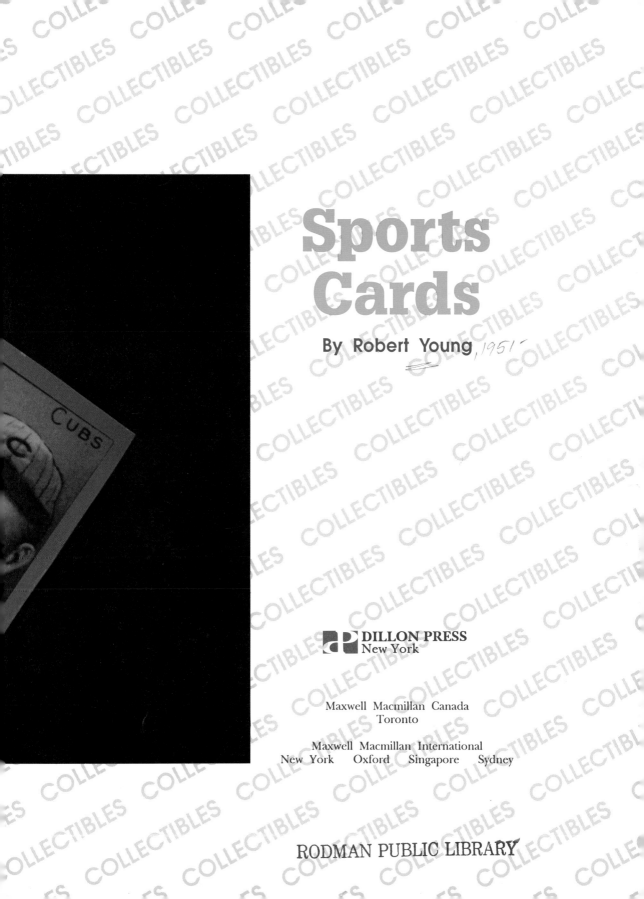

DILLON PRESS
New York

Maxwell Macmillan Canada
Toronto

Maxwell Macmillan International
New York   Oxford   Singapore   Sydney

For Peggy,
an all-star Mom

Acknowledgments

With many thanks to the following people for their generous help: Timm Boyle, Susan Finley, Larry Fritsch, Bill Guilfoile, Steen Graham, Erik Herskind, Jason Jackson-Berger, Janet Jacobsen, Dave Kelts, Doug Koke, Pat LaFond, Chuck Liska, Pat Lissy, Jay McCracken, Allen Maine, Gary Meininger, Wes Morgan, Jason Nugent, Bill O'Connor, Steve Riley, Eric Rohde, Jenna Rohde, Gene Sanchez, Tucker Smith, Joyce Stanton, Jill Sternthal, Marty West, Nelson Wheeler, George White, Gary Yoshimura, Sara Young, and Tyler Young.

Photo Credits

Cover: Robert Young
Back Cover: Robert Young
Robert Young: Half-title page, title page, 6, 9, 12, 16, 19, 35, 36, 38, 50, 56, 60; Upper Deck: 14, 59; Baseball Hall of Fame: 21; The Metropolitan Museum of Art: 23; Dave Kelts: 24, 28, 32; Skybox International: 40; Topps: 46, 48

Book design by Carol Matsuyama

Library of Congress Cataloging-in-Publication Data

Young, Robert, 1951-
    Sports cards / by Robert Young. — 1st ed.
       p. cm. — (Collectibles)
    Summary: Discusses the history, production, and collecting of trading cards featuring people in sports, a hobby on which Americans spend a billlion dollars a year.
    ISBN 0-87518-519-3
    1. Sports cards—Collectors and collecting—Juvenile literature. (1. Sports cards.)
I. Title. II. Series: Collectibles.
GV568.5.Y56   1993
769'.49796—dc20   92-33761

Dillon Press
Macmillan Publishing Company
866 Third Avenue
New York, NY 10022

Maxwell Macmillan Canada, Inc.
1200 Eglinton Avenue East
Suite 200
Don Mills, Ontario M3C 3N1

Macmillan Publishing Company is part of the Maxwell Communication Group of Companies.

First edition

Printed in the United States of America

10 9 8 7 6 5 4 3 2 1

CONTENTS

CHAPTER 1

Millions and Millions of Cards

If you like sports and are interested in collecting, you're in luck. For you, there are millions of opportunities. They come in the form of small cards made of thick paper. On the fronts are pictures of people in sports. On the backs are more pictures as well as information about the people. These paper treasures are trading cards known as sports cards.

At first they were simple prizes placed in tobacco products. But it didn't stay that way. Other companies saw how well sports cards helped sell their products. This led to a long list of companies that used sports cards to help sell their products over the years. Sports cards have been included with everything from chewing gum to dog food.

For most of sports cards history, very few choices were offered to buyers. There were a couple of types of cards to collect, but mainly there were baseball cards. Now things are different. Much different. Sports cards has grown into a $1 billion a year

The millions of sports cards available today come in many sizes and styles.

industry with more than 25 million Americans buying sports cards each year.

Baseball is clearly the most popular type of sports cards, followed by football, basketball, and hockey. But these aren't the only sports cards made and sold. There are many more, including cards that focus on car racing, horse racing, golf, boxing, lacrosse, skateboarding, soccer, surfing, tennis, volleyball, and wrestling. There are cards of minor league players, Olympic athletes, and college players. There are cards of cartoon characters with superstars. You can even get a sports card made of yourself, whether you're a superstar or not!

And don't think that all sports cards are the same size and shape or that they have only writing and pictures on them. Cards come in several sizes and shapes. There are Braille cards for blind collectors, talking cards so you can hear a player's voice, cards that glow in the dark, and "scratch 'n' sniff" cards.

Sports cards aren't the only types of trading cards you can buy and collect. There is a trading card for people with just about any possible interest. There are trading cards that feature cartoon and comic book characters, criminals, dogs, dolls, explorers, fire trucks, movie and TV characters, musicians, and

Of the four most popular types of sports cards, baseball takes the lead, followed by football, basketball, and hockey.

wars. In some cities trading cards of police officers are given out so that kids will get to know them better.

Nonsports cards are becoming more popular every year. But even though sales of nonsports cards grew by 300 percent between 1990 and 1991, they still were only 15 percent of the trading card market. The other 85 percent of the market belonged to sports cards.

Who collects sports cards? All kinds of people. Boys collect cards. Girls do, too. So do adults, both men and women. Each person has his or her own reason for being a collector.

Some collect sports cards to learn more about the people and events of a sport they enjoy. Others collect sports cards to make money. And then there are the people who collect for the joy of collecting.

Although reasons for collecting may be different, the result is that sports card collecting is one of the fastest-growing hobbies around. If you doubt that, just look around you. It won't take much looking to see the evidence. Sports cards are sold in all kinds of stores. There are card clubs, books and magazines about cards, as well as card shows and conventions. Sports cards are even put into museums.

The National Baseball Hall of Fame and Museum in Cooperstown, New York, opened in 1939 and was the first museum devoted to a sport. The museum is best known for its displays that show the history of baseball. But the museum also displays a collection of baseball cards. This exhibit contains more than 900 cards, from 1887 to the present.

Because the Baseball Hall of Fame and Museum brings so many visitors to Cooperstown, a collector decided to open his own museum there. Larry Fritsch had been collecting baseball cards since 1948. To help support his hobby, he started a mail-order baseball card business in his spare time. By 1970 his mail-order business had grown so much that Fritsch quit his full-time job to sell cards. This made him the first full-time sports card dealer.

Fritsch continued to collect cards as well as sell them. By the end of the 1980s he had more than 34 million baseball cards in stock for sale. The cards in his personal collection—which he never sold—numbered over one million and included complete sets by manufacturer of almost every year.

To share his giant collection with others, Fritsch opened the Larry Fritsch Baseball Card Museum in 1988. On display are 20,000 cards, from 1948 to 1990.

The most famous collection of sports cards is part of a larger collection of paper collectibles. It includes not only sports cards but also other trading cards as well as greeting cards, postcards, and valentines. It is the collection of Jefferson Burdick and it is kept in the Metropolitan Museum of Art in New York City.

Jefferson Burdick, born in 1900, began collecting cards around 1910. He collected sports cards and every other kind of card he could get his hands on. By the 1930s Burdick had a huge collection of cards. He also had a lot of knowledge about cards so he began writing articles about card collecting. Soon he was publishing his own newsletter called *The Card Collector Bulletin*.

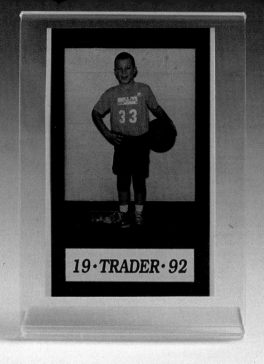

You can even have a sports card made of yourself!

In 1939 Burdick began producing a catalog, which he updated for some 20 years, to help collectors know what cards were available. To help organize the hobby, he created a system that identified cards by categories. He used a letter or letters to indicate how or when the cards were issued. This was followed by a number for each set. A few examples of the letters he used are:

> T —20th-century tobacco cards
> E —Early candy and gum cards
> D —Bakery cards
> W—**Strip cards,* exhibit cards**, team issues
> H —Advertising cards

*Words in **bold type** are explained in the glossary at the end of this book.

By 1947 Burdick had one of the largest card collections in the world. He offered to donate it to the Metropolitan Museum of Art, and the museum accepted. To make the cards easier to display, Burdick decided to mount them in albums. But there were 300,000 items to mount and Burdick had a bad case of arthritis, which made it difficult for him to use his hands.

From 1948 to 1963 Burdick slowly worked on gluing and pasting his cards into albums. Even though his health was getting worse, Burdick kept working until all 394 albums were filled. Two months later he died.

If Jefferson Burdick were alive today, he would probably be pleased at how many people are collecting sports cards and at how organized many collectors are. But because he worked hard at keeping the price of cards low, he would most likely be concerned at the value of cards today.

Collectors want cards today, and when that happens, the price for cards goes up. Sometimes the price goes way up. Consider the former New York Yankee star Mickey Mantle's 1952 Topps card. Its value jumped from $3,000 in 1988 to $8,000 in 1990. By 1991 the same card sold for more than $50,000. And, of course, there's the most valuable

In 1991 hockey star Wayne Gretzky became a part-owner of a valuable Honus Wagner card.

sports card ever: the early 1900s card of Pittsburgh Pirate shortstop Honus Wagner. In 1980 the card was valued at around $3,000. By 1988 the value had increased to $30,000. The next year the card sold for $115,000. In 1991 hockey star Wayne Gretzky and Los Angeles Kings owner Bruce McNall bought a Honus Wagner card at an auction for $451,000!

The rising prices of sports cards have made millionaires of some collectors. They've also made criminals of people trying to get rich by counterfeiting cards. How is it that these small paper cards have come to be so valuable? Let's start from the beginning. . . .

- In 1991 six out of every ten trading cards sold were baseball cards.

- Fourteen percent of United States households have a sports card collector in them.

- About 10 percent of all the people in the United States buy sports cards each year.

- Males outnumber females in sports card collecting by four to one.

- Car racing cards aren't always sports cards. If the drivers are pictured on the cards, they are sports cards. If cars are pictured, they are nonsports cards.

- Not all people pictured on sports cards are athletes. When the National Hockey League teams chose local heroes to be celebrity captains in 1992, cards of these people were made by Pro Set. Celebrity captains included TV star Mr. Rogers, actor James Belushi, and actress Susan Saint James. Saint James was the first woman to appear on a hockey card.

- The Larry Fritsch Baseball Card Museum was the first baseball card museum.

- Between 1980 and 1990 the number of people collecting sports cards increased by about 600 percent. The number of dealers increased by 1000 percent.

CHAPTER 2

Early
Sports Cards

The history of sports cards begins with an unlikely subject: tobacco. In the late 1800s America was quickly becoming **industrialized**. That means many different products were being mass-produced in factories with the help of machines. One of those products was cigarettes.

Before machines were used, cigarettes were rolled by hand. Companies could make cigarettes faster and more cheaply by using machines. Tobacco products soon became popular, and many companies started to profit from the growing number of people using these products.

Because of the large number of companies, selling tobacco products became very competitive. Companies had to find ways to get people to buy their products. One way they did this was by including **premiums**. A premium is a small prize that comes with a product. Some companies decided to use cards as premiums. The cards were pictures glued to cardboard. They were about three times as thick

These early sports cards were used as premiums—prizes inserted in packages of gum and cigarettes.

as the cards made today.

The idea of using cards as premiums wasn't new. Advertising cards—which were handed to customers—had been used in the United States. Tobacco companies in England had been putting cards in their products for years. Their cards included pictures of animals, flags, and war heroes.

In the late 1880s several tobacco companies in the United States began using cards as premiums. The Allen & Ginter Company of Richmond, Virginia, included sports cards in its packs of cigarettes. These cards featured many kinds of sports stars of the day, including baseball players, boxers, oarsmen, and wrestlers. The popularity of the cards helped to sell the products. They also helped stiffen the flimsy packages.

Another cigarette manufacturer, Goodwin & Company, decided to focus on baseball cards as premiums for its Old Judge and Gypsy Queen cigarette brands. The reason was that baseball was quickly becoming a national sport, with teams being started in cities across the country. Between 1887 and 1890 Goodwin issued cards of more than 500 different baseball players, both major and minor leaguers. These were the first sets of cards that focused purely on baseball.

Early sports cards were smaller than the cards manufactured today. Most were about 1½ by 2½ inches. Some of the cards had copies of colorful paintings printed on them but most were photographs. Photographers took pictures of players in studios, printed them on yellowish brown photographic paper, and then glued them to pieces of cardboard.

As competition grew among tobacco companies, new types of cards were made. **Cabinet cards** were larger cards that measured about 4½ by 6½ inches. These cards were designed to be displayed

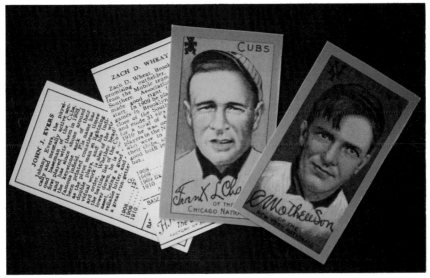

Tobacco cards were smaller than modern sports cards. They measured about 1½ by 2½ inches and had information about the players on the backs.

on cabinets in people's homes. They were too large to be put into packages of tobacco products, so companies included coupons that could be exchanged for these cards. Tobacco companies continued to use sports cards as premiums until the mid-1890s. That was the time when large tobacco companies bought smaller tobacco companies. Suddenly, fewer companies were competing to sell tobacco products. Manufacturers didn't have to offer premiums to get people to buy their products. As a result, for about ten years not many sports cards were made.

That changed in the early 1900s when new companies began importing tobacco from Turkey. These companies began offering cards as premiums once more, and they created cards of many different sizes and shapes. Some had gold borders, others had several players pictured on them. Most were baseball cards, although there were a few hockey cards being produced.

The American Tobacco Company issued one of the most famous sets of cards between 1909 and 1911. This set, the T-206, is made up of baseball cards featuring more than 500 different major and minor league players. Several cards in the set are

Cabinet cards on display in the Baseball Hall of Fame

worth a lot of money because of mistakes. Joe Doyle, who was a pitcher for New York's American League team, was incorrectly identified as playing for the National League New York team. Sherry Magee, an outfielder for Philadelphia, had his name misspelled as Magie on the card. The printing plate for Eddie Plank's card was damaged. The plate was not fixed or replaced, so not many cards were made. Eddie Plank was a star pitcher for Philadelphia's American League team.

The most valuable card of the T-206 set is the Honus Wagner card. Wagner, whose real name was John Peter Wagner, was one of the most popular players of the day. He played shortstop for Pittsburgh and later became a member of the Hall of Fame.

There are two different stories to explain why there are so few Wagner cards. One story is that Wagner demanded his card not be sold because he was opposed to smoking and did not want to promote it in any way. Another story has it that Wagner was angry that he wasn't paid for appearing on the cards. In any event, the American Tobacco Company took the Wagner card off the market, but not before some had already been sold. It is believed that fewer than 40 cards still exist.

The famous Honus Wagner card, the most valuable card of the T-206 set

In 1911 Mecca created one of the first sets of baseball cards with player statistics on the backs. These cards, called **doublefolders,** used a flip-up design so that two different players could be shown on each card. The next year Hassan came out with interesting new cards called **triplefolders.** These cards pictured two players that could be folded over an action scene.

Soon other industries were realizing that baseball cards could help sell their products. Candy companies

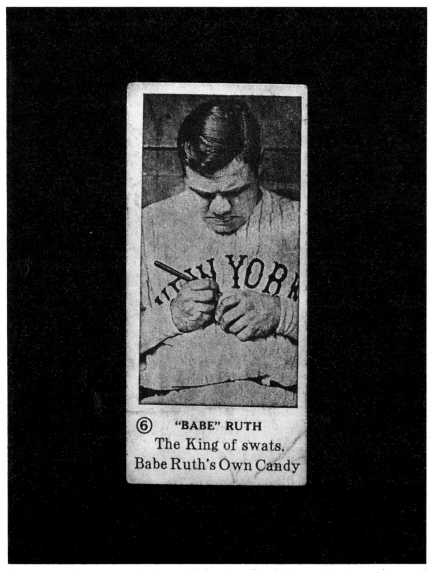

⑥ "BABE" RUTH
The King of swats.
Babe Ruth's Own Candy

Soon candy companies were following the tobacco companies and offering cards as premiums.

used cards as premiums. So did bread companies, chewing gum companies, and magazines. They printed baseball cards on a variety of materials, including felt, leather, and silk.

Making sports cards came to a quick halt in 1917 when the United States entered World War I. Materials as well as factories were needed to help in the war effort. Cards were not made again until the early 1920s.

With New York Yankee star Babe Ruth playing, the 1920s was a great time for baseball. Surprisingly, it was not a great time for baseball cards. The government divided up the large tobacco companies, making many small producers of tobacco products. These companies chose to promote their products in ways other than using premiums. This left the use of cards as premiums mainly to candy companies.

But sports cards were not only used as premiums in the 1920s. Some, called exhibit cards, were sold in vending machines. Others were sold in stores as strips. Strip cards are color drawings of players that were printed on strips of thin cardboard or heavy paper. They were designed to be cut apart by store owners or by people who bought them.

In the late 1920s a product came along that

was important in the history of sports cards. In 1928 Walter Diemer, an accountant for the Fleer Corporation, invented bubble gum. Bubble gum was not only an interesting new product—it was a great match for sports cards.

It wasn't long before other companies were making bubble gum, too. The Goudey Gum Company included Big League cards with its bubble gum in 1933. National Chicle Company sold its gum with a series of cards called Diamond Stars. Gum, Inc., which had made the first set of football cards in 1935, became the leading card producer in 1939 with its Play Ball series of baseball cards. With the help of these companies, cards became known as "bubble gum cards."

But then along came another world war. And as before, the government needed materials and factories to help in the war effort. So in 1941 most companies stopped making sports cards. It looked as if it would be the end for sports cards forever. But it wasn't. Not by a long shot.

- Players often wore makeup to get their pictures taken for early cards.

- Not all early cards were sports cards. Allen & Ginter made cards of famous people such as Buffalo Bill and Annie Oakley.

- By 1891 Goodwin & Company had featured more than 700 baseball players on 2,300 different varieties of cards.

- The T-206 card set is known as "The Monster" to many card collectors. It is made up of about 7,500 different cards.

- In the mid-1920s Cracker Jack made cards in which color could be added by brushing water on them.

- In 1933 the Goudey Gum Company did not include card number 106, Napoleon Lajoie, in its baseball card set. It was said that Goudey did this so kids would keep buying their gum to get the missing card. After many letters of complaint, the company issued the card in 1934 and sent a free card to everyone who had written.

- By World War II the Collins-McCarthy Candy Company had been producing cards for 28 years, longer than any other company.

- There were 15 to 20 times more tobacco baseball cards made than tobacco hockey cards.

A 1953 Bowman card. That was the year the company first used color photographs instead of hand-colored black-and-white pictures.

CHAPTER 3

Modern Sports Cards

When World War II ended in 1945, most card companies did not start making cards again right away. Materials needed to make the cards were still in short supply. It took another three years before cards were being produced in the quantities they were before the war.

In 1948 Bowman Gum Company, which was once Gum, Inc., produced sets of baseball, basketball, and football cards to go with its Blony bubble gum. These cards were 2 1/8 by 2 1/2 inches with a black-and-white photograph on the front. On the back was the card number as well as the player's name, team, position, and a short biography.

Other companies began to compete with Bowman that same year. Topps came out with a card set called Magic Photos. The fronts of these cards were blank but then developed into black-and-white photographs when they were taken from the pack and exposed to light. In addition to baseball players, the cards in this set featured dogs, movie stars, track stars, and war heroes. These cards were sold with

Topps's Bazooka bubble gum.

Chicago's Leaf Gum Company also issued a set of baseball cards that year. The cards, 98 to a set, had black-and-white photographs that had been hand-colored.

Bowman learned from its competition. In 1949 the company colored the black-and-white photos in its set of 240 baseball cards. Bowman also began signing major league players to **exclusive** contracts. If a player signed an exclusive contract with a gum company, that meant his picture could not be placed on cards issued with gum from any other company. By signing many players to exclusive contracts, Bowman was able to almost eliminate its competition. But not for long.

In 1951 Topps issued four different sets of cards, three of which were baseball cards. One set was of major league teams; another featured Hall of Fame players such as New York Yankee stars Babe Ruth and Lou Gehrig. The other set of baseball cards were both picture cards and a game.

It wasn't long before gum companies realized they could make more money selling cards than gum. Soon the battle was on between Bowman and Topps. Each wanted to sell more baseball cards than the other. To do this, Topps began trying to sign on players to exclusive contracts. Bowman improved the pictures on its cards. Topps made its cards larger and added color. Bowman used color photographs instead of coloring black-and-white pictures. Topps added player **statistics** on the card backs. Bowman made cards with more than one player on them. Both companies made their sets of cards larger, and both changed the designs of their cards.

By 1955 Topps had signed most major league stars to exclusive contracts. This made it difficult for Bowman to sell its cards and stay in business. The battle between Bowman and Topps was over. The next year Topps bought out Bowman.

The improvements that came to sports cards as Bowman and Topps competed helped make cards more popular in the 1950s. Because of that popularity, baseball cards were issued as premiums with many products in different regions of the country. The products included breakfast cereal, cookies, hot dogs, potato chips, and even dog food!

You might think that because baseball cards were so popular, other sports cards would be popular, too. But that's not right at all. Baseball cards were so popular because baseball was the most

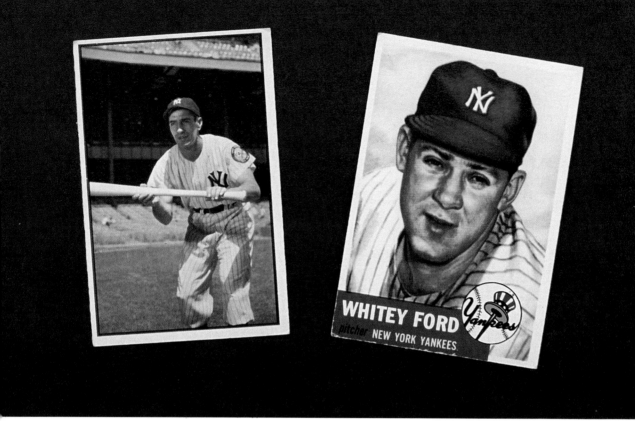

Bowman (left) and Topps (right) waged a long hard battle to see which company could sell more baseball cards.

popular sport in the United States in the 1950s. Topps tried making sets of basketball, football, and hockey cards during that time, but they did not sell nearly as well as baseball cards.

After 1956 Topps controlled the baseball card market. The company did this by signing most major league players—and many minor league players—to exclusive contracts. Some companies, like Fleer and Leaf, tried to compete with Topps, but they had to make cards of retired players or sell their cards with products other than gum.

It was easier for Fleer to compete with Topps in making other kinds of sports cards than to change its product line. By 1961 Fleer had tried making both basketball and football cards. Still, baseball cards were the most profitable area of sports cards. What Fleer really wanted to do was make baseball cards.

It took nearly 20 years before Fleer and other companies would be able to make baseball cards. Fleer took Topps to court in 1975, charging the company with illegally preventing other companies from making and selling baseball cards. When the decision was given on July 1, 1980, the judge ruled in favor of Fleer. Fleer and other companies were free to issue baseball cards with their gum.

Fleer immediately began producing baseball cards. So did Donruss, a Tennessee company that had been making nonsports cards since the early 1960s. Both companies issued a set of baseball cards with gum in 1981.

Topps decided to appeal the 1980 ruling. The company took its case to a higher court and this time it won. The court stated that Topps had exclusive contracts to issue baseball cards. The ruling, in fact, went even further: Only Topps could issue cards alone or with gum.

Donruss and Fleer had to stop issuing baseball cards with gum, but they didn't have to stop making and selling cards. So, starting in 1982, Fleer included a sticker that had a team **logo** in each pack of baseball cards. Donruss included puzzle pieces in each of its.

Many changes came to sports cards in the 1980s. New companies began making cards. In 1986 Sportflics created Magic Motion baseball cards. Each of these cards had three different pictures on the front that could be seen by tilting the card. In 1988 Score came out with a set of 660 baseball cards with color photographs on both sides. The packaging was clear so you could see the cards inside.

In 1989 Upper Deck produced its first set of baseball cards. The 800 cards in this set brought more changes to the industry. They had excellent action photographs printed on white card stock, giving them a crisp, high-quality look. They also had features to prevent some of the problems of card collecting at the time. Some people were opening packs, taking out higher value cards, replacing them with cards of lower value, and resealing the packs. To prevent this, Upper Deck put its cards in packages that could not be resealed. To prevent counterfeiting, the company

Donruss, trying to compete with Topps, included puzzle pieces in its packs of baseball cards.

placed a small **hologram** on each card. In addition, each pack came with a card-sized hologram.

Also in 1989, LJN Toys, along with Topps, made the first talking sports cards. These large-size baseball cards had miniature records on the backs. When the cards were put into special record players, the ball player's voice could be heard.

Many new types of card sets were developed in the 1980s. These included sets that were given away at ballparks as well as sets distributed by police and

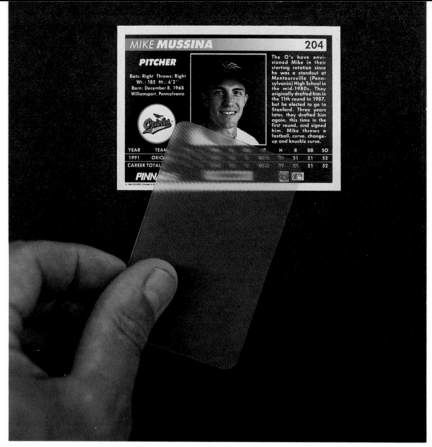

To prevent counterfeiting, Score prints its name at the bottom of its cards. The name can only be seen by holding a special piece of plastic over it.

fire departments. You could buy special-edition sets, boxed sets, or sets of cards that featured only traded players.

With so many cards on the market, millions of people got involved in collecting them. During the 1980s card collecting grew by 20 percent each year, making it one of the fastest-growing hobbies. It wasn't long before other types of sports cards became popular, too.

The popularity of football cards increased when the National Football League teamed up with a company to produce cards. In 1989 Pro Set issued a 440-card set of "official" NFL football cards. By working with the NFL, Pro Set was able to have access to the league's pictures as well as its writers. The result was improvements in the quality of football cards. By the end of the 1980s, one-fourth of sports cards sold were football cards.

Interest in basketball cards grew, too. Following the NFL in 1989, the National Basketball Association teamed up with a company named Impel and produced NBA Hoops cards. The next year the NBA and Impel began making Skybox cards as well. Skybox cards are premium, high-tech cards with backgrounds created by computers. In 1992 Impel changed its name to Skybox International and continued to make and sell both Skybox and NBA Hoops cards.

Sales of hockey cards rose during this time, too. This was the result of both the growing interest in card collecting as well as the popularity of players such as Wayne Gretzky and Mario Lemieux.

The great interest in collecting sports cards has brought about changes. Some of them have not been so good. Older cards are more expensive because so many people want them. And with all the new cards coming out, it is just about impossible to collect them all. Figuring out what to collect can be very confusing.

But not all the changes have been bad. Because there are so many cards made today, new ones are easy to get. You can buy them just about anywhere, including through the mail. You can attend sports card shows every weekend and read about sports cards every day of the week. There is no shortage of information about sports cards. And that is good news for collectors.

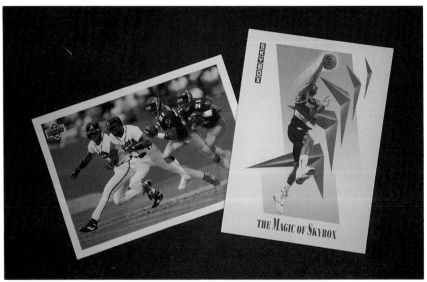

Today some card companies are using high-tech manufacturing methods. Upper Deck's card of Deion Sanders (left) shows four views at once of the baseball-football player. Skybox (right) used computer graphics to create the background for its glossy basketball card of Buck Williams.

- In 1949 the Bowman Gum Company produced a set of baseball cards that showed players from the Pacific Coast League. This was the first set of minor league cards made by a national company.

- Color photographs were first used on sports cards in 1953 by Bowman.

- Bowman featured umpires on its cards in 1955.

- Topps was the first company to feature rookie stars on its baseball cards in 1959.

- In 1974 Topps began releasing its set of cards all at once. Before then, it had released only a part of its set every couple of weeks throughout the season.

- In 1989 Topps produced a set of Bowman cards to attract collectors who liked the original Bowman cards.

- In 1990 Upper Deck became the first major company to put personally autographed cards in some of its packs.

- Because of collector complaints, Topps began issuing cards without gum in 1991—the gum left marks on the cards.

Designs for new cards often are created on computers.

CHAPTER 4

Making
Sports Cards

Sports cards may be small and look simple, but they are not easy to make. It takes machines, money, and people working together to make sports cards.

Before sports cards can be made, a company has to decide what types of cards it is going to make. If the company is small, the owner decides. For larger companies, there are many different ways for decisions to be made. In some large companies, a committee is made up of managers from several departments such as advertising, art, marketing, new products, and sales.

The committee discusses ideas for new sets of cards. In considering an idea, several questions are asked: Are there similar cards being sold already? How many people will buy the cards? What kind of profit could be made selling the cards? Research is done to find answers to these questions. If the answers look good, the committee gives its approval for the cards to be produced.

There is one big step that must be taken before

any sports cards can be made. The company must get a **license**, or official permission, to make the cards. The company applies to the league so that team names, uniforms, and logos can be used. It also applies to the players' association so that pictures of the players can be used. If the license is approved, the company must then pay a lot of money, sometimes millions of dollars, to the league and the players.

Once the card company gets the license, it can start making cards. The first step in making sports cards is the design. The committee that approved the cards sends its ideas to the art department. There, with the help of computers, designers use that information to create the look of the card set.

Designers have many decisions to make. They have to decide what size and style of lettering to use on the card as well as what colors to use, what kind of border, and where to include players' positions, team logos, and other information.

Designers are very busy. Not only do they create the designs for new types of sports cards a company is making, but they also update existing sets of cards every year. The reason most card designs are changed each year is simple: It creates continued interest in the cards. Changing card designs also helps collectors quickly identify the year the cards came out.

Designers create several different sample cards, called mock-ups. These cards are shown to the manager committee, which then decides what design to use.

After the design is chosen, it is time to put the cards together. Workers in the photo department pick out the best pictures of each player. The workers have thousands of slides from which to choose. Photographers have been working all season long getting shots of all the players.

The photos may be the most important part of sports cards, but the writing is important, too. It is the writing that tells important information about the pictured player. Writers at the card companies get their information from many different sources, including the league as well as private companies that collect sports information. Some writers keep file cards on each of the players, highlighting notes, quotes, facts, and figures.

The card design, photographs, and text are all entered into computers. The computers scan the colors of the cards and create film negatives. There are negatives made for each of the four colors used in printing: yellow, **cyan** (greenish blue), **magenta** (purplish red), and black. These four colors are combined to create all other colors. All full-color illustrations are printed using just these four colors. The reason four different negatives must be made is that each of the colors must be printed separately, each one on top of the other, forming layers of ink. Each layer of ink is broken up into small dots of different sizes. If you look at a sports card through a magnifying glass, you will see dots of the four printing colors all mixed together. Color pictures in books and magazines are also printed in the same way.

Each of the negatives is combined with 100 or more others and taped onto big plastic sheets called **flats**. Each flat has negatives for one of the four colors on it. A "window" is cut in the plastic behind each negative so that light can pass through only the area of the negative that is supposed to print.

Each flat is placed into a frame along with a printing plate, which is a thin piece of aluminum that has a special light-sensitive coating. The flat and plate are pressed together and exposed to strong light. The light passes through the windows of the negatives and onto the plate. These are the image areas of the plate, and the chemical coating on them makes them receptive to the inks. The light is not able to pass through the dark areas of the negatives or the plastic.

When each plate is developed, it contains all the images from the negatives that were on the film flat used to make the plate. One plate is made for each of the four colors. When all four color plates are made of both the fronts and backs of the cards, printing can begin.

The plates are checked and then taken to a printing press, where they are each attached to a large metal **cylinder**. Each cylinder will print one of the four colors of the cards. As the cylinder turns, water is applied to the plate. The water sticks to the background of the plate but not to the image areas. The press then spreads one color of ink onto the plate. The ink is oily and it sticks only to the image areas of the plate. Since water and oil do not mix, the water rolls off the oily ink and stays only on the areas of the plate that do not print.

As the cylinder turns, it presses up against another cylinder. This cylinder has a rubber coating, which picks up the ink from the plate. The rubber cylinder then prints the images onto thick sheets of paper that have been fed into the printing press.

Cards are printed on large thick sheets of paper.

The sheets of paper are pulled through the press to the three other cylinders, and as they pass through each they are printed with the other main colors. When the first sheet of paper has been completely printed with all four colors, it is carefully checked to make sure the colors are correct. A worker can easily change any color by simply pushing buttons. The buttons control the amount of ink being put on the plate cylinder.

When the colors are correct, a large stack of paper is automatically fed into the presses to print thousands of cards. But only one side of the cards is printed at this time. When all the fronts of the cards are printed, the sheets of cards are stacked on platforms with wheels. They are left to sit for between 18 to 36 hours to let the ink completely dry.

When the ink has dried, workers wheel the platforms to the front of the press again. The sheets of paper are turned over and put in place so they can be fed into the press. Press operators put printing plates on that show the backs of the cards. The presses are started and the backs of the cards are completed.

After the ink has had a chance to dry on the backs of the cards, the sheets are taken to a cutting machine, which cuts them into smaller sheets. Another machine mixes the smaller sheets of cards. This is done to make sure the same cards won't be packaged together.

Mixed sheets of cards are inspected before they are put into another machine that trims the edges and then cuts them into individual cards. Workers then put these cards into a machine called a pocket feeder. The pocket feeder is made up of several pockets in which cards are automatically stacked. Bonus cards are placed into the stacks as well as special, autographed cards that some companies use. The pocket feeder pulls cards from each of the stacks until it has enough cards to make up a pack. An electronic eye checks to see if the correct number of cards has been pulled for each pack.

Groups of cards now enter the wrapper, which automatically wraps them into packs. The cards can be wrapped in many different materials, but usually waxed paper, cellophane, or foil is used. The wrapped packs of cards are boxed and sealed. Then they are shipped to stores and dealers in places wherever collectors want them. And that's just about everywhere!

The final step: Wrapped packs of cards are boxed, ready to be shipped.

- Pro Set pays photographers $200 for the front and back images used on its football cards.

- Companies are very careful in choosing the photographs to put on their sports cards. Upper Deck uses fewer than 1 percent of the photographs that people send in.

- The blades of the cutting machines at Pro Set are changed twice each day to make sure the card edges will be sharp.

- Sports cards that do not pass inspection are shredded at the card factory.

- Topps makes more than one billion sports cards a year.

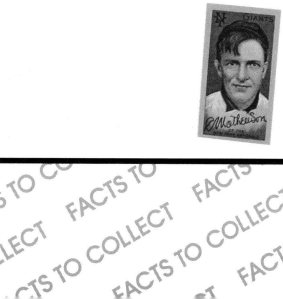

SPORTS CARDS

You can find sports cards in many places. Some shops, like this one, sell only sports cards.

CHAPTER 5

Collecting
Sports Cards

Collecting sports cards can be easy and fun. Just make sure to remember one thing: You can't collect them all. That's right, there are too many sports cards to collect. Over the years, billions have been made. If you were lucky enough to be able to find them all—which would be almost impossible—there is no way you could afford to buy them all.

And then there's today's sports cards. More sports cards are being made today than ever before. There are more than 200 different sets of baseball cards alone made every year.

Since you can't possibly collect all sports cards, choose an area on which to focus your attention. Do you have a favorite sport? If you do, try collecting cards of people who play that sport.

That's just one way to focus your collection. There are many other ways. You can collect cards of your favorite players or your favorite teams. You can collect cards made by a certain manufacturer or produced in a specific year, such as the year you were born.

Some people collect only rookie cards. A rookie card is the first card of a player in a regular set made by a major manufacturer. Other people collect only error cards, which are cards that have mistakes on them. Cards of superstar players are another popular group to collect. You can also collect **commons**, which are cards of nonsuperstar players.

When you are deciding what kinds of cards to collect, keep in mind how much money you have and are willing to pay for your collection. Cards of popular players usually cost more; so do older cards, rookie cards, and any other cards lots of people want.

Once you have decided what kinds of cards you want to collect, it's time to build your collection. Where should you start looking for cards? That's easy. Start looking in your own house. Kids often buy cards, then put them in a box or a drawer and forget about them. If you find cards that you don't want to put in your collection, don't throw them away. You can give them away or trade them for cards you want.

After you've checked around your house, ask people in your family if they have any sports cards. Don't stop with your immediate family, either. Ask your cousins, aunts, uncles, and grandparents if they have any cards available. Relatives might have cards stored away. Tell them you are starting a collection, and let them know what you're looking for.

There are many places to get sports cards. Besides stores that sell only sports cards, you can buy new cards in convenience stores, drugstores, hobby stores, supermarkets, and toy stores. Sports card shows are good places to buy cards, too. Check your local paper or sports card magazines for listings that tell when and where the shows will be held. Sports card magazines also have ads that tell where you can buy cards through the mail.

Other places to look for sports cards include antique stores, flea markets, garage sales, and swap meets. Sometimes you can get cards for bargain prices at these places, but you have to be careful. The people selling cards at these places often don't know a lot about sports cards. That means they could be asking more than a fair price.

How do you know what a fair price is? Well, that depends on what player is pictured on the card, how old the card is, and how many were made. It also depends on the condition of the card.

To help set a fair price, collectors grade the

condition of a sports card. Grading provides a general guide to the condition of a card. The different grades include:

Mint (M or MT)—A card in perfect condition. The colors are bright and clear, the corners are sharp, the pictures and writing are centered, and there are no marks on the card.

Excellent (E or EX)—Shows light wear or minor defects. Corners or edges are not sharp, borders are slightly uneven, or the cards have wear that you can only see by looking closely.

Very Good (VG)—A card that has been handled but not abused. Some rounding of the corners, nicks in the edges, borders that are turning yellow or brown, or light creases.

Good (G)—A well-handled card. Corners are rounded and layered (paper separated in layers), or the card is deeply creased. There may be holes or writing on the card, and possibly tape or paste marks.

Fair (F)—A heavily worn or damaged card. Corners are rounded, layered, and sometimes torn; edges are frayed; borders are dirty; several deep creases; and colors are faded. Often has holes or writing on it, or tape marks that have removed some of the printing.

Poor (P)—A card that has been abused. Areas are missing because of tearing or trimming, large holes, water damage, or other serious abuse. These cards are often only collected until a better-grade copy can be bought.

Look at the card closely to determine its grade. Then use a price guide, such as those published by Beckett Publications, to figure the value of a card. Remember, though, grading sports cards is not a perfect system. Two people might grade the same card differently.

Grading cards and using a price guide makes it easier to trade with other collectors. Figure out the current value for the cards you are willing to trade. Use those prices to make sure you are both getting an equal value of cards in the trade.

As you build your collection, it is important to take good care of it. That way, you will be able to enjoy your cards longer. It will also mean more money for you if you ever choose to sell them.

Use good sense when storing your cards. Keep them in a dry place that is neither very hot nor very cold. Never leave them in direct sunlight because that might cause the colors to fade. Put your cards in something to protect them.

When you want to trade or sell your cards, it helps to check a price guide.

If you store your cards in a box, use a box that is about the same size as the cards. By stuffing the extra space with cloth or cardboard, you can prevent the cards from sliding around and becoming damaged.

Another way to store your cards is in albums, such as three-ring binders. There are many kinds of three-ring binders; some are made especially for storing trading cards. They are built sturdy to handle the weight of the cards. They also have rings designed so the pages of cards will lie flat.

Many collectors slide their cards into special pages made of plastic. These pages, as well as the binders, are available in hobby and sports card shops as well as at card shows and through mail-order catalogs. To avoid damaging your cards, put only one card in each pocket. Be careful when buying pages for your cards; in the past a chemical called **polyvinylchloride** (PVC) was used in making plastic pages. Collectors found that PVC leaked from the plastic pages and left an oily mark on the cards.

Most companies making plastic pages today use chemicals other than PVC. Still, it is best to look carefully at plastic pages before you buy them. Hold them up to the light. Can you see rainbow colors in the plastic? If you can, that means chemicals are leaking. Another way to find out if there is leaking is by feeling the plastic. If it feels greasy, that's another sign that leaking is taking place.

Organize your collection in a way that makes sense to you. It might be by year, by team, by sport, by favorite players, or another way you have created. After you have your cards organized, take some time to page through your albums and enjoy them.

There are other ways to get enjoyment from your sports card collection. Many people think it is fun to display their favorite cards. You can buy many different products to display your cards. They range from individual plastic holders to picture frames to show your favorite players.

Autographed cards are fun to display, too. Send cards to some of your favorite players. Make sure you have extra cards of those players because some will not sign or return your card. Often it's the superstar players who won't respond because they get too many requests. Try sending to players who aren't superstars and you will have a better chance of getting a response.

Write to the players in care of their teams. You can get the addresses of all professional teams from the *World Almanac* at your library. Include a short, polite letter requesting the player to sign and return your card. Make sure to enclose a stamped, self-addressed envelope.

There are lots of things to do with your sports cards. You can use the information and statistics to learn about players and sports. You can also play with your cards. One of the oldest games is card flipping. Before the game starts, decide whether cards won will be kept or not. In one variation of this game, two players each hold a card in the

Autographed cards are fun to have in your collection. Here, Baseball Hall of Famer Lou Brock signs a stack of his cards.

Card flipping, a favorite pastime for many collectors

palms of their hands. At the same time, both players flip their palms over and let the cards drop to the ground. The player whose card lands "heads up" wins the other player's card. If both players' cards are heads, they flip again.

Another flipping game is played by tilting a card up against a wall. Players take turns trying to knock the card down by throwing other cards at it. The player who knocks the card down wins all the cards on the ground.

You can play games of baseball with your baseball cards. Design a field right on the living room floor using books for fences, paper bases, and foul lines made of string. Place your baseball cards on the field in the correct positions, then pitch a small foil ball to yourself and hit it with a pencil bat. If the ball hits one of the cards in the field, the batter is out. If the ball falls between the cards, you decide what kind of hit it is.

These are just a sample of games you can play with sports cards. What kinds of games can you create? Just remember that playing with your cards will most likely cause some damage to them. Because of that, you might want to use doubles with which to play.

So what happens when you get tired of collecting sports cards? What should you do then? One thing you can do is to sell some or all of your cards. Before you sell any, make sure you know what they're worth. Then you can sell them to a friend, take them to a dealer or card show, or put an ad in the paper.

Another thing to do if you want to stop collecting is to put your cards away for a while. Maybe you'll get interested again in a couple of years. Maybe you'll forget about your cards for a long time. When you discover them again, they will remind you of the time when you collected. They also might just be worth a lot of money!

- The value of Topps sets of the 1960s baseball cards increased by 15 to 16 percent between 1988 and 1989. Topps 1970s sets increased more than 23 percent during that time.

- Computer programs are made that help people organize and keep track of their sports card collections.

- **Checklists** are important cards in completing a set. They are most valuable when they are clear and unmarked.

- Cards of superstar players are worth from 10 to 20 times more than the cards of common players from the same set.

- Twenty-eight percent of all sports cards are sold in convenience stores.

- In April 1992 a 12-year-old boy in Stockton Springs, Maine, found an old tobacco can while raking leaves. Inside the can was a T-206 Honus Wagner card. Although the card is badly creased and faded, it is still worth between $15,000 and $40,000.

SPORTS CARD TIME LINE

1871 —The first professional baseball league is formed

1887 —Tobacco companies begin including sports cards with their products

1909 —The American Tobacco Company begins to issue its T-206 set of baseball cards

1911 —The Mecca Company creates doublefolders, the first cards with statistics on the backs

1912 —Hassan Cigarettes produces triplefolders, folding cards that show two players and an action scene

1917 —World War I brings card making to a stop

early —Card making begins; candy companies
1920s make more cards than tobacco companies

1928 —Fleer's Walter Diemer invents bubble gum

1933 —The Goudey Gum Company starts selling cards with its gum

1934 —National Chicle sells its gum with a series of cards called Diamond Stars

1935 —National Chicle produces a set of football cards

1941 —World War II slows card making

1947 —Jefferson Burdick donates his card collection to the Metropolitan Museum of Art

1948 —Bowman Gum Company produces sets of baseball, basketball, and football cards to go with its Blony bubble gum; Topps introduces its Magic Photos card set; Leaf issues 98-card sets of baseball cards

1949 —Bowman adds color to its cards; begins signing players to exclusive contracts

1951 —Topps issues four different sets of cards; begins competing with Bowman for exclusive player contracts

1953 —Bowman is the first company to use color photos on its cards

1954 —Topps issues its first hockey card set

1956 —Topps buys Bowman; controls the card market

1957 —Topps makes its first set of basketball cards

1961 —Fleer enters basketball card market

1980 —Fleer wins lawsuit against Topps; Fleer and

Donruss begin making baseball cards

1982 —Topps wins appeal; Fleer and Donruss have to put something other than gum with their cards

1986 —Sportflics makes Magic Motion cards

1988 —Score issues a set of 660 baseball cards with color photos on both sides; Larry Fritsch opens the Larry Fritsch Baseball Card Museum in Cooperstown, New York

1989 —Upper Deck produces a set of baseball cards with holograms on them taking card making to a new level; LJN Toys and Topps make talking sports cards; Pro Set teams up with the NFL to make a 440-card set of football cards; Impel teams up with the NBA to make basketball cards

1990 —Impel uses computer graphics to produce Skybox basketball cards; Upper Deck starts including personally autographed cards in some of its packs; Reggie Jackson's was the first

1991 —Topps stops including gum with most of its packs of cards; Wayne Gretzky and Bruce McNall buy a Honus Wagner T-206 card for $451,000 at an auction

FOR MORE INFORMATION

For more information about sports cards and particular brands, contact:

Collect-A-Card Corp.
P.O. Box 17588
Greenville, SC   29606

Fleer Corp.
10th and Somerville Streets
Philadelphia, PA   19141

Leaf, Inc.
P.O. Box 634
Memphis, TN   38101
(Donruss)

Major League Marketing
25 Ford Road
Westport, CT   06880
(Score, Sportflics)

Pacific Trading Cards, Inc.
18424 Highway 99
Lynnwood, WA   98307

Pro Set, Inc.
17250 Dallas Parkway
Dallas, TX   75248

Skybox International
2510 Meridian Parkway
P.O. Box 14930
Research Triangle Park, NC
27709
(NBA Hoops and Skybox)

Topps Company, Inc.
254 36th Street
Brooklyn, NY   11232

The Upper Deck Company
5909 Sea Otter Place
Carlsbad, CA   92008

For more information about sports card magazines, write to:

Allan Kaye's Sports Cards News & Price Guide
10300 Watson Road
St. Louis, MO   63127

Pro Set Gazette
17250 Dallas Parkway
Dallas, TX   75248

Topps Magazine
P.O. Box 555
Mt. Morris, IL   61054-0555

Trading Cards
Suite 300
9171 Wilshire Boulevard
Beverly Hills, CA   90210

Tuff Stuff
2309 Hungary Road
Richmond, VA   23228

For more information about sports card clubs, write to:

Front Row Collectors Club
P.O. Box 37
Dalton, PA   18414

Club Pro Set
1-800-258-2099
(Ask your teacher to call for a
catalog.)

Places to visit:

The Larry Fritsch Baseball
Card Museum
10 Chestnut Street
P.O. Box 150
Cooperstown, NY   13326

The National Baseball Hall
of Fame and Museum
Main Street
P.O. Box 590
Cooperstown, NY   13326

Metropolitan Museum of Art
1000 Fifth Avenue
New York, NY   10028
(the Burdick collection)

GLOSSARY

cabinet cards—cards that were larger than usual and used for display

checklists—numbered or alphabetical lists of cards in a set

common—the card of a nonsuperstar player

cyan (sy-ANN)—a greenish blue color

cylinder (SIL-in-der)—a long, round object

doublefolders—cards that used a flip-up design so that two different players could be shown

exclusive (iks-KLOO-sive)—not shared with others

exhibit cards—cards sold in vending machines

flat—a plastic sheet used in printing

hologram (HO-luh-gram)—patterns of laser light recorded like pictures; they create images that are three-dimensional

industrialized (in-DUS-tree-a-lized)—using machines and factories to mass-produce products

license—official permission

logo—symbol

magenta (ma-JENT-ah)—a purplish red color

mint—perfect condition

polyvinylchloride (pol-ee-VINE-ul-KLOR-ide)—a chemical used in making plastics

premium (PREE-me-um)—a small prize that comes with a product

statistics (sta-TIS-tiks)—numbers, facts, and other information that are collected about a particular subject, like a baseball player

strip cards—color drawings of players printed on heavy paper or cardboard and sold in strips

triplefolders—folding cards that showed two players and an action scene

INDEX

ABOUT THE AUTHOR

A fourth-grade teacher and free-lance writer, Robert Young is fascinated by kids and the things they collect. In addition to the books in the Collectibles series, Mr. Young has written about a wide range of subjects. *The Chewing Gum Book* and *Sneakers: The Shoes We Choose!* are two of his titles recently published under the Dillon Press imprint. Mr. Young lives with his family in Eugene, Oregon, and enjoys visiting schools and talking to teachers and students about writing.